BRIEF

LANDING

Hall

SURFACE

THE BRITTINGHAM PRIZE IN POETRY

The University of Wisconsin Press Poetry Series
Ronald Wallace, General Editor

Places/Everyone • Jim Daniels
C. K. Williams, Judge, 1985

Talking to Strangers • Patricia Dobler
Maxine Kumin, Judge, 1986

Saving the Young Men of Vienna • David Kirby
Mona Van Duyn, Judge, 1987

ocket Sundial • Lisa Zeidner
Charles Wright, Judge, 1988

Slow Joy • Stefanie Marlis
Gerald Stern, Judge, 1989

Level Green • Judith Vollmer
Mary Oliver, Judge, 1990

Salt • Renée Ashley
Donald Finkel, Judge, 1991

Sweet Ruin • Tony Hoagland
Donald Justice, Judge, 1992

The Red Virgin: A Poem of Simone Weil • Stephanie Strickland
Lisel Mueller, Judge, 1993

The Unbeliever • Lisa Lewis
Henry Taylor, Judge, 1994

Old & New Testaments • Lynn Powell
Carolyn Kizer, Judge, 1995

Brief Landing on the Earth's Surface • Juanita Brunk
Philip Levine, Judge, 1996

BRIEF

LANDING ON

THE EARTH'S

SURFACE

Juanita Brunk

THE UNIVERSITY OF WISCONSIN PRESS

The University of Wisconsin Press
114 North Murray Street
Madison, Wisconsin 53715

3 Henrietta Street
London WC2E 8LU, England

5   4   3   2   1

Printed in the United States of America

LIBRARY OF CONGRESS CATALOGING-IN-PUBLICATION DATA
Brunk, Juanita.
    Brief landing on the Earth's surface / Juanita Brunk.
    64 pp.   cm.—(The Brittingham prize in poetry)
    ISBN 0-299-15200-6 (cloth: alk. paper).
    ISBN 0-299-15204-9 (paper: alk. paper)
  I. Title. II. Series
  PS3552.R7999B75   1996
  811'.54—dc20   96-15118

ACKNOWLEDGMENTS

Thanks to the editors of the following magazines, in which these poems first appeared:

The American Poetry Review: "Green Waters," "Leaving Crete," "This World," "Valentine"
Cimarron Review: "In April," "I Used to be Unbelievably Sexy"
Passages North: "Mrs. Richards Plays a Starlight Waltz," "On This Earth," "Anniversary,"
    "Flood," "Infidelity"
Poet Lore: "All Sweet Things, Like Forgiveness, Are a Falling," "Bleeding-Heart," "Can,"
    "Carrot," "Heartbreak," "My Father's Tongue"
Southern Poetry Review: "Fortune"

I am grateful to the Wisconsin Institute for a fellowship which supported me during the writing of some of these poems. I would also like to thank the Mary Roberts Rinehart Fund.

Many people helped in the making of this book. I would like to mention Peter Klappert and Brad Burkholder; and I would especially like to thank Debra Nystrom, Kelly Cherry, Gary Young, and C. K. Williams for their generous attention to the manuscript. For their loving interest in its progress, thanks to my parents. Above all, for his unwavering encouragement and support, I am deeply grateful to Todd London.

FOR TODD AND GUTHRIE

CONTENTS

O, but it happens every day

To someone. Suddenly the way

Leads straight into their native lands,

The *temenos'* small wicket stands

Wide open, shining at the centre

The well of life, and they may enter.

W. H. AUDEN

New Year Letter

I

This World

Today, still dazed and unsteady
from last night's dream, I carry my coffee
to the porch: there was a war; I was shuttled away
on a flatbed truck from everyone,
the ones I love.
But here the day is already steamy, the sun
breathing down on the concrete steps, the morning glories
wide open, unfurled and perfect in their extravagant blueness,
crowded as germs on a vine that has wrapped itself
entirely around the railing and onto the roof.
They seem to come from a different world,
they are so blue, and so many,
but here they are,
hundreds of them, every blossom a raised glass,
every blossom a throat. They drink the light
and change it: sky. I have a friend
with eyes this shade of blue.
I think about her
and the way she talks, the way her voice speeds up,
climbs higher, cracking, as if you're being taken from her
even as she speaks, as if she had to reach you somewhere far away,
she's that excited. Last time I saw her she was standing
on a moving bus, unsteady, hanging on, but waving,
waving, blowing kisses, until the Greyhound
had completely turned the corner
and was gone.
Then I think about another time, a boy,
in Crete. My room was in the hills, but every day
I walked or hitchhiked to a village by the ocean, and that day
when a bus went by, a load of children, one boy waved
and I waved back. And would have forgotten
except that hours later, in the village

in a shop where I was buying plums,
a woman was crying, her eyes darker than the fruit,
one thumb lifting her apron
to smear away tears while she counted out change.
Outside the sunlight glinted in the market square as if the stone
were full of broken glass, and I went back
to where my friends were sitting,
a cafe where we'd started meeting every afternoon
for wine or ouzo: a boy from Germany, two girls from Sweden,
me. We hardly spoke, just sat together, drinking,
watching the merchants arrange
and rearrange their racks
of colored scarves
and bulky handmade sweaters.
When I got back some news had come around:
a small boy, in the village on a field trip
with his schoolmates, was swimming
in the ocean when the current
pulled him under. This had happened
in the last half-hour: the current pulled him down
and he was dead. Marta, telling us the story, had understood
no more than that. After a time two women walked by,
wailing, voluminous in skirts and head shawls,
and then the children, a row
of tiny stoics holding hands, no one
pushing or shoving anyone else, no one quarreling
or crying. We were so close to them
we could have touched them, and we were far away from home,
the separate countries where, like drawers of clothing
in our parents' houses, our own real lives
had seemed to wait. But then,
as much as to our families
or our lovers, more, we seemed connected to each other,
bound by the rickety enamel table, by the crumbs,
the half-drunk bottle of retsina,
flickering, cast by sunlight onto Gunter's arm,
bound, even, by our lack of grief, our sense of being,

4

for whatever curious reason, left behind.
I thought of the way I imagined the Second Coming
as a child, how I would see myself returning home from school
to find my family spirited away, lifted in an instant
from the earth, the house empty,
nothing to note my mother's place but a potholder, dropped,
or, rolling across the floor, a slowly unravelling spool of thread.
I thought of the boy's mother sending him off that day,
kissing his hair as, pleased and excited,
he clutched the bag
that held his swimming trunks and towel.
And I thought of the bus on the road, the hand, grown smaller,
larger now, in memory, waving.
Maybe not even the same boy.
That was ten years ago.
He would be eighteen or twenty by now
and I would be thirty, on a porch in Madison, Wisconsin,
so tired I want to go inside the house and back to bed.
I want to sleep again, remembering my mother
who is still alive,
and my friend with eyes like flowers,
and the boy, and Günter, and the others, who are by now
deep into whatever life they have made.
I want to wake up again
to this world, this time a throat, wide open,
this time one of many, on a vine, shouting, for one day
before they shrink to tiny fists,
to wizened purple:
oh, blue, blue world, a cup of light
we have to drink, our potion,
a morning holding out its glory.

II

Anniversary

Winter: a day so foggy
the world ended where the neighboring fields
began. Days of rain and cold
had turned the lawn to hardened clay.
I carried the garbage out
over the frozen path to the incinerator.
The bag was damp and splitting open;
I clutched it to myself.
Crumpled on top was paper
from a florist, a bright, unnatural green.

Match after match,
I leaned into the odor
of our sodden trash, wet grapefruit rinds
and tissues and envelopes smeared with coffee grinds
spilled across a pile of unburnable debris:
tin cans, bits of foil and plastic,
a child's small metal car
half buried in ash.
Only the paper flared easily.

Inside, we sat down to eat
without speaking. Later, the fog would thicken
and surround the house, travelling in
the way it does, until the eye
succumbs, no longer trying
to reconcile that blankness
with an image, landscape or face,
of what you think you saw.

He Comes Home

He comes home blue,
in a pouch of cold air. When you move close
its folds are the hard ribs
of an oyster shell.

There is no cracking it open.

Inside, his milky nub of sadness.
If you listen, you can hear the noises
of his heart,
sucking it clean.

Can

Losing you is a tin can
clinking against a barbed wire fence
in the middle of the night.
A farmer with piss on his pants
tied it there and laid it open with his shotgun
late one Saturday, drunk and with nothing inside
to talk to but the linoleum floor.
Now someone in a neighboring house can't sleep
and is lying awake listening
to it clatter, not constantly,
but whenever the wind knocks it around.
After awhile it will be morning,
and I can get up, and light will come in,
not the kind that makes the world look large
and possible, but the kind a camera uses
to turn an event into chemicals
and paper, reduced,
so you can file it in a drawer
or frame it: small tin can,
small fence, small farmer.

Flood

The baby blooms beside me
on the cross-town bus, powdered skin
and laundered bunting,
someone else's creampuff.
I haven't combed my hair today or washed my face,
still raw from last night's quarrel.
The problem: I won't move in,
or leave my clothes at his place.
What weary stuff. Truth is, I'm lacking.
There are times when just a sentence
changes the whole story
and rearranges all that's come before.
I long for that upheaval. Call it a warm spell
early in the season: water floods the house.
The kitchen table, liberated,
floats across a vanished lawn.
It must be similar to being born,
the old surroundings turned mysterious and new.
A miracle, or maybe just what happens.
The little stranger, for example,
perched here beside me in this funny world,
fist curled, patting her toothless gums.
Each time the bus hits a pothole
her eyes open wide, each time,
again and again, luminous, surprised.

Infidelity

The story they create is more compelling
than any book, and with what variety they dream
of its conclusion. At this stage it is clear as light;
there will be an undoing. In separate rooms
they imagine lifting off
their clothes, sweaters and stockings
fallen to the floor with the soft clamor
of pages turning, a graceful unravelling of plot.

They call it fire,
an act of nature ruining their houses.
As though it didn't begin with hands and matches
in a corner of the cellar, a closet
full of rags and gas cans and furniture from the past,
a place where some small light seems essential,
so far away from the comings and goings
of the family upstairs,
a damp and hungry pocket
where those familiar voices
call and call and can scarcely be heard.

After the Garden

When we woke stunned, cast out,
sunk back into our selves, rooted, foot,
ankle, mud, every grain
and molecule set
on the path toward dissolution,
we wanted nothing but to be taken.
Let the mites that would feast on our skin
day after day have us completely.
Let whatever force had fashioned us
deliver us entirely back to clay.
Not to wait,
not to be abandoned here
with only the tedium of our own flesh
to keep us company, blistered hands mashed
from the till, our mouths plastered together
in boredom and despair as much as love,
our sex-cries plaintive as loons
as we begat a race
of refugees,
tribe after tribe of our kind,
the memory and scent of our homeland
passed down, that longing to return
embedded in them like a gene,
the ghostly, insatiable itch
of a lost limb.

In April

The retarded couple in the house next door
is having a fight. It's finally spring, the windows
are open, and from the porch I can hear them
over the noise of a radio and the sound
of a baby crying.
I can't tell what they're saying
but I hear the histrionic climb of their voices
and the way they're locked in anger.
I sit on the porch, smoking and listening.
There are two measly crocuses
that have come up next to the sidewalk.
They've rooted through the mud and mashed-down grass
but they're barely distinguishable from the ground itself,
they're so small and ragged. Now I hear thumping
and banging, and the sound of things being thrown.
Her voice is eerie, out-of-control;
she's really wailing.

He stomps from the house
in an exaggerated huff. He's got an old piece of cloth
in his hand, a rag or torn blanket, and as he walks
he slaps it against the ground. His corduroys
have slipped down past his waist,
past the clump of white flesh
his T-shirt doesn't cover.
He goes as far as the street
and stands there, slapping the rag at a torn flyer
that's been taped to the telephone pole,
working it loose.

Now the screen door slams
and she comes after him, crying,
large in anklets and heavy shoes,
her red hair greasy and plastered with barrettes.
She lunges toward him and begins pummelling his back
until he turns around,
his arms loose,
the muddy whip hanging limp
at his side. He looks lost and scared,
and then, maybe because they're here, outside,
everything shifts, and he starts crying, too.

They're on the ground now; she's straddling him.
They've got their arms around each other,
crying and rocking and blubbering.
They don't care that I'm barely six yards away,
or that other neighbors, too, have stopped to watch,
that we're all a part of it:
his head mashed against her chest,
his stubby fingers spread
and moving on her wide haunch
as if riveted to the one thing
not yet lost.

Vale of Tears

But there is an hour
like this: you would cry for weeks
to have it. You sit so quietly

you are a hand, lying palm up.
Red coals percolate in the fireplace, heat
seeps through the walls of the house. In the next room
someone slips butter into a hot pan.

All day it has been raining.
All day you have heard the rain falling
against the windows and wanted nothing but that.

You see how intricate the path?
Every stroke is luck that brought you here, the afternoon
not a breath away, but alighting, its visible plumage
no longer distinguishable from your own.

Valentine

It doesn't matter that sooner or later
the line of my throat will come between us,
and the set of your jaw will come between us,
blueprints of smoke in the bedroom
and no high racket in the stars.
And it doesn't matter that sooner or later
my words will be wrong words, they will ruin your food,
they will sift through your body like sand,
you will grow leaden with the weight,
you will be a dumb bag
holding back floods.
And then I'll dance so close to him
I might as well have fucked him, and you will dance
so close you might as well, and I'll wish I hadn't
and I'll wish I had, and you will be desert
and I will be cracking and parched.
And the worms that live in our skin will start eating
their way out, there will be spots on the crests of our backs,
spots in the rub and burn of our bellies,
on the smooth linen of your cock,
in the silky oysters of my earlobes,
we will be mottled as leopards and it won't be lovely,
it will be stinking and zoo. And it doesn't matter
that one evening sooner than late
over bratwurst and schnitzel
a fat German frau
will start schlumpfing around in your head
and a Nazi will microphone cues in my voicebox
and bigots and racists will waltz on the sheets
where we once made love. And men from my past will begin
to arrive, and one will take my clothes
and one will take my name,

and then my eyes will go, and then my voice,
after awhile I'll have no arms, no feet,
my legs will be sore stubs,
I'll barely be able to writhe my way to the ward
to be mended, it will take months,
it will take years.
And when you come to visit me,
when you stand at the door of my room
all rosy and separate and shaved,
I'll see wreck, I'll see accident,
and when you look at me you won't see fiesta,
you won't see meat and potatoes,
you'll see one stingy tube
of sugar water
drip, dripping from a vein.
Heart, it doesn't matter that shadows
lie coiled in our armpits, that they rise up
and follow us, that they love us more than our bodies,
right now it's night. They're sleeping.
Right now the moon is as fine
as a baby's fingernail up in the sky
and a tiny thread hangs from the hem of a long black skirt,
one tug and it all unravels,
one tug and I'm naked, it's Christmas,
it's Valentine's Day, it's March,
it's April, it's Halloween.

III

Green Waters

Today the air is so heavy
the trees barely move, as if their weight
of new leaves were the green weight
of a stilled pond,
thick with algae, beneath the surface
a galaxy of cells exploding. Beyond these windows,
past the green waters of the trees, everything happens
at once, even another day, where under a trellis
of hibiscus and bougainvillea an old man
rolls his sleeves and stretches
for an afternoon siesta,
his brown face closing inward
to the place where memories, gold fin
against fin, swim beneath a latticework of shadows.
Or imagine a girl, a green heat
moving through her
for the first time, all the rich cells
of her life to come such an explosion within
that she knows, though she has been waiting and preening
for months, how little it has to do with this boy,
leaning against her in the darkness,
or his hand, stroking, slower
and slower now, the skin of her suddenly
stilled and rapturous face.

Bleeding-Heart

for Muriel Dimen

Pink, split open,
the heart-shaped body
of the flower sways on its delicate stem
with the burdened grace of a testicle
and spills, from its torn red tip,
a sequestered self.
This seed
or chip of gravel
hangs in a sac, a ruptured membrane,
as if the rebel, still attached,
drags with it as it goes
the milky, bleeding center
of its nest.

On This Earth

To love my own, my body,
to know without saying, *legs, you are good legs,*
and feet and stomach and arms, good, and the spaces
under my arms, and the brown pigments
splashed across my back like tea leaves.
To love my body the way
I sometimes love a stranger's: a woman
on the subway, tired, holding her two bags,
a child slumped against her like another sack
as the train stops and starts and the child says something
so quietly no one else can hear it,
but she leans down, and whispers back,
and the child curls closer. I would love my body
the way a mother can love her child, or the way
a child will love anyone
who gives it a home on this earth, a place
without which it would be nothing, a dry branch
at the window of a lit room.

Letter to Myself as a Child

You wake to birdcalls,
your mother's footsteps down the hallway
past your door. *Amazing grace,*
she sings, her arms piled high with laundry.
Sunlight warms your face
and dawdles in the sheets. You rise, dress,
leave the house as if on urgent business.
Barefoot, you leap across high grasses
in the field, drag the dinghy through mud,
throw in a life preserver
that you never wear
and row south, past the duck blinds
and buoys that mean *deep water,*
past the sandbar.

The house is small in the landscape.
As though you were already gone, you dream a little
of your life there, but what you think of mostly
is the way this river leads into a larger river,
bay, then ocean. The sun beats down
on your skin, warm and brown,
and you lift the oars
into the hull
and lay a palm against your belly,
stroke your thigh. *Amazing grace,*
deep water. The tide turns
your drifting boat toward the river's mouth
and, further, toward a flickering spot of white,
so tiny and uncertain
it's barely more than premonition,
a gull's wing or a sail
reflecting light.

Carrot

I grow in darkness,
toward the center,
what some people call Hell.
I eat mud. I look like a penis,
but I am all mouth.
My leaves are delicate, the lie
I show the world. It takes two hands
to pull me from the ground,
my home, my private suck.

My Father's Tongue

My father could not say the words.
They were heavy as bricks or lumber;
they took the shape of stairways, scaffolding,
buckets of stucco or concrete.
They multiplied,
became buildings with rooms and puttied windows,
walls braced and sheathed to hold in heat
or hold a whisper out, doors
that could be slammed.
They were the clothing strangers left
in a ditch, reeking and stiff, crusty trousers
that he found and carried home in cardboard boxes,
rank woolen jackets waterlogged
with mud and soot,
heavy coats that shrank
in the washer and shed chunks
of gritty lining in our clean socks and underwear.
They were the neighbors' discarded appliances
salvaged on trash day and piled up
in our basement to be fixed:
hair dryers with melted innards, doll carriages
without wheels, lamps with frazzled cords
and dangling necks.
The things my father couldn't tell us
were cars that stuttered and broke down
by the side of the road,
nothing to do but stop
and see if you can make it right,
his hands with wrench or crowbar or hammer
battered from trying to make us hear,
one thumbnail always bruised
or growing back.

All Sweet Things, Like Forgiveness, Are a Falling

Think of cushions on a sofa
in the house where you lived as a child.
Evenings when you settled there your head grew heavy,
dropped, and you left behind the grievances
and clutter of the day, let your arms
and legs go slack and undemanding,
losing will. You drifted
from your body, from the room
with its cumbersome chairs like sentries
and lamps that puddled light onto the dark creases
of your father's face and onto your mother's hair
where she sat, sewing. How simply you fell,
spiralling gracefully downward
into shifting territories
of light and undiscovered languages
you understood. And if you woke or half-woke
later, you heard the clink of dishes as someone set the table
for tomorrow's breakfast, your own milk mug
at your place. A distant pulse,
the household carried on
as you were lifted, carried;
voices—*the window, Ruth*—sheets drawn
around you, a lamp clicked off.
All sweet things happen
in that place where, once more, you are falling,
holding nothing, holding nothing back. In a far province
a tailor catches light on his needle
and weaves it into clothes that you will wear.
Bells are being cast to wake you.
A feast. A land peopled
with strange faces you will grow to love.

Fortune

His hands are like potatoes
warmed in the oven all day. Nothing delicate
about them. Not only that
but he cooks potatoes. I come into the house
and the lights are on; he's there in the kitchen
and those hands are holding a small wooden knife
and cutting up potatoes, red potatoes, white;
he's wearing his comfortable pants
with the roomy waist and something simmering smells
like I've gone my whole life without eating anything
that matters compared to that.
Outside it's cold and inside I feel
my good fortune growing the way a potato
swells in the ground, at home with its territory,
no need for fancy green shoots, anytime
you burrow, there it absolutely is.

Where My Mother Cries

It is always November, the driveway lined with gold,
the air rich with the smell of burning leaves.
Other years she placed the brightest leaves in silver bowls
with evergreens and mums; the house
was sweet with autumn. In order not to ruin
a picture I've made for her at school, a woman

and a girl, I walk carefully. The woman
is tall, her hair a fury of gold.
The two are smiling in the face of ruin:
trees with black leaves,
a burning house,
smoke drifting in a capsized bowl

of sky. I know the sky is not really a bowl.
It goes on forever, like time, that will change me to a woman,
claiming everything. I enter the dark house.
In the kitchen, a row of pots gleams gold
against the wall. I leave
my jacket on a hook, neatly, as if ruin

did not live here, as if ruin
were not a dark bowl
my mother has fallen into, and will not leave.
She seems like someone else, another woman
with her skin, her eyes, her brown hair shot with gold
and gray. She is not at home in this house

though she sits in the house
all day in a ruin
of yarn, knits a scarf the muddy gold
of mustard, grows thin, will not eat from the bowls
of soup my father offers. Once a woman
begins to leave

she might leave
everything, her house,
her children. Once the woman
recognizes ruin,
it might be everywhere, in someone's hands, or in a bowl
of soup, the rich broth yellow as fool's gold.

Where my mother cries, a woman gathers autumn leaves.
They look like gold, or summer's ruin.
The silver bowls are mine. There is no house.

Papaya: Lancaster County

Inside the Amish health food store
Mattie, the eldest daughter, stuffs wedges
of papaya into plastic bags and fastens them
with rubber bands, the thick brown braids
of her hair tied back
beneath a bonnet. I think about papaya,
swinging in fat globes on the trees of a country
she'll never visit, being harvested by people
she might struggle to imagine,
and of the way it's sliced
and dried and shipped
across an ocean to end up
in her hands in this dim store
where a wooden sign says
Miller's Food. Horse Ties in Back. No Photography, Please;
and the clocks are never changed to daylight saving.
It's early, only seven-thirty, standard time.
Later, tourists will come
with cameras and brochures
and photograph her weighing onions,
slicing cheese. But now, her face inscrutable
and calm, she moves among shelves of almonds and pine nuts,
herbal teas and remedies that reek of hay.
She nods, but we don't speak.
We're strangers, really.
I know nothing
of what she does or doesn't long for.
If we meet at all it's through the dumb heaviness
of fruit, lifted from palm to palm,
our fingerprints joining in the bright flesh
of the papaya, the puckered skin of the prune.

Leaving Crete

In the third-class berth an old man
moans, and turns in his sleep. He stinks of ouzo,
sausage, sweaty clothes. The ferry bucks and groans
toward Athens, but in his dream he's travelling back
to Kamilari on a bus, past olive groves
and graveyards where the dead are buried beneath relics,
things they love, photographs and little bottles,
a wooden flute preserved in glass.
It rattles into villages
where goats and chickens scuttle
from the road and drying trousers on a line
are tangled by the winds from Mirtos, lush with fragrances
of dittany and quince. Home! the old man cries
but then the bus is gone and he is walking,
entering a room where sunlight thins
in corners dark with permanent dust. He dreams
of waking in an iron cot but in his waking he is carried
deeper into sleep. He turns again, moans,
his mouth against the vinyl bunk,
a ticket in his pocket. Outside the porthole
the sea swallows islands as they pass: slabs of white rock
dissolve, fold into black.

At Thirty-Four

Suppose it were alright
to be small, no bigger than a leaf
or the shadow of a leaf,
silent,
not the letter
but the seal.

IV

Mrs. Richards Plays a Starlight Waltz

There's a Buick dealership
where her house squatted in a clutter
of ceramic statues: a jockey
hoisting a lantern, elves and mushrooms
clustered around a birdbath full of rotting leaves,
a salmon-pink flamingo. Seven, I carry an empty lunchbox
past a spruce still draped with Christmas bulbs,
onto the porch where the purple clematis
dangles its weird, white-rimmed blooms.
Inside is sudden darkness.
Pale and fat, she sits by the piano, bare arms
like buoys, her girdle and wig removed
for comfort, red hair gone to fuzz.

I play my piece, "A Starlight Waltz,"
pounding her baby grand the way at home
I pound our toneless spinet. Now the cuckoo
pops out to perform
his mysterious office, bows three times
and chortles, bobs back in. She grumbles,
shifts. Then softly, as one would touch a stranger
or a lover, her fingers brush the keys.
On a veranda lit by moon and stars,
this century or another,
a man bends toward a woman, the notes
around them drifting, moving on.

I think of science class,
the day the teacher brought a jar
of lilac-scented cream. She carefully opened it
to show us that a fragrance, though unseen,
is particles of something real.
Released, it travels through the air like pollen,
through the screens and into traffic,
farther, beyond our houses,
yards, the swing sets, jungle gyms,
the things we know;
beyond the edge of town,
the tall and temporary trees.

My Father Waits on the Banks of the Warwick River, 1939; My Mother Returns from a Picnic

The boy rowing the boat is not important.
The one who matters is leaning with one shoulder
against a tree, a stalk of grass between his teeth,
his shoes polished.

He watches the oars that lift
and spill the river, fall
and lift. As the boat swings north
the girl takes shape, her dress
a darker blue than sky
or water.

The girl pretends she doesn't see him
waiting there, legs crossed, his white shirt
streaked with shadows. She bends
and reaches for a metal thermos bottle
full of tea.

One oar scrapes bottom, mud and shell.
Between them now is only shallow river water,
scattered foam, a strip of sand. The humid air
is spongy with the smell of marsh.
They breathe it in,
exhale.

At Hilltop Manor

for a great-uncle

Because you live at the end of the street,
your garden is in the wrong place. You think
it happened when they changed the locks.
They say, *That's Florence's room,*
That's Florence's room. That room is taken.

Your heart is beating.
Something has gone terribly awry.
You tell them the woman is not your wife.

There are building permits that were never sent;
two loads of lumber that have been derailed.
And this was where you plowed
and planted. You walk in circles
looking for the spot.

When you finally find it,
nothing has come up. Or everything came up,
corn, beets, parsley, lettuce,
but someone stripped it, picked it
clean, down to the last pale green shoot.

Hear that Dog Barking?
He Wants to Get into Your Poem

Once rabbits were my all.
I lived for their delicate whiff,
sniffed for miles, followed sweet-scented scrub
bush to bush, sifted through leaf and brush
in meadows of quitch for rank pockets
where those riff-raff twitchers hid,
dreamt of the sharp white grip
on wily rabbit flesh,
pithy and tufted.

Now they've gone simple,
dull as heifers in a stubbled field.
Who even wants them, skittering beneath
this excellent nose?
These days, I favor barking. That, too,
I still do well. I bark at caterpillars, squirrels,
the moon advancing bit by bit above the hill.
Hear me barking? Write it down.
Move in for the kill.

Living without You

Another spring.
The same birds returning
ride in like gusts of blowing paper,
shrill beaks shredding air.
I walk down the sidewalk
repeating: sparrow,
starling, crow.
On the ground
sloughed tulip petals sidle
back and forth, still breathing,
their awful purple smeared
with yellow pollen.

The Ancient Emperor Mourns His Sugar Baby

Come back as a gnat to poke
with your enameled thorn, come back
a bruised banana, mad monkey, the farting croak
that billows from a frog. Come back
as anything but smoke.
Come back as Rose Red and I won't give you
to my brother, come back a bag lady,
ballerina, purple shoe. Come back a country
music singer, strike a pose. Come back
a black and scarlet pigeon,
kitchen clock, wilting pink
rose. Come back lost in the dryer,
my stray striped sock. Come back the goodwife,
I, woodman, will leave the pudding, long and bulbous
as a cock, on the end of my nose.
You can have the third wish.
Come back a yellow dress,
a fish, opening like a tulip, swallowing
my hook. I'll be the fisherman
drinking beer on the dock.
Come back a crook.
Come back an upper lip, I'll ride you,
stiff hair of the mustache. Come back a wrinkle,
rusty lock, a violet sash that I'll undo
as you have me, a fat old Chinaman
blubbering while you turn
to ash, an emperor,
inconsolable, crying in my tea.

Immaculate Conception, 1969

On the church steps
after evening service
when Larry Fisher crams his tongue
into my mouth, I press my legs together
and angle them away,
knowing neither skirt nor cotton panties
are obstacle enough to save me.
Potent and otherworldy forces
have inhabited my body;
masses of sperm shimmy headlong
to my newly magnetic crotch. *Teen* magazine
has confirmed it: they can travel through clothing,
especially when damp. Maybe Joseph and Mary
were simply swimming, or battling
the same strange tides
that I am now, while,
in the fields behind the church
the shadowy cows barely move, and I sink
and rise, sink and rise, a sea,
a Bermuda Triangle, able,
miraculously,
to absorb whole ships full of tourists
on their hapless, determined way
toward tropical bliss.

Cooking the Lobster

I imagine this lobster
lying on my analyst's couch.
Her elegant red pincers sway lightly
as she speaks. *I don't feel safe here,*
she says. Soon she will be weeping
steamy tears. I plunge her in,
but I remember Albert Schweitzer,
carefully catching house flies
and setting them free.
Even the chardonnay!
So many migrant workers,
barely paid.
And for what? My moment
of well-being, a split second
when, after a forkful of lobster
slick with melted butter (mouth-feel
is what food scientists call it, why
we like warm fat), in front
of a noisy fire
on this cold night in winter,
one sip is all I want,
a moment of satisfaction,
half of it, at least, for what is not:
I am not outside tonight,
not hungry, not dead.

When You Woke Crying

Because you woke crying
two birds leaped from one tree
to another, a cloud passed over.
I climbed a ladder of sleep
but you were not there.
The sky was far too big
and all the trees in the forest
were infested and dying,
but I remembered your name
and stumbled to your crib.

Because you woke crying
shadows flickered at the window
and wolves lined up at the door.
They wanted to make you one of them.
In the dark I picked you up
and you grew quiet,
and I held your small white feet
in my hands and buried my nose
in the folds of your neck.
With your sharp tiny teeth
on my skin, you bit a perfect O,
but I held you close. It was up to me
to teach you human ways.

Rock-a-bye, rock-a-bye,
at my breast you murmured pleasure.
Oh, the winds from Siberia were cold,
my darling. The oceans slopped debris.
But under the blanket
your heart thumped mightily.
Who knew what would happen next?
In the night air, we made a space.
We sprouted leaves,
one here, one there.
This is the way we would grow
for a few more years.

Heartbreak

A pigeon
walks with bound feet
along a precipice;
the next minute, gone.

There will always be a moment
that I will miss

when, on the next street, a girl
in an orange flared skirt
steps from a shop;
the wind lifts her skirt

as it grows dark,
as the rain gathers
and begins
in the city where I love

her polka-dot kerchief
from another time

though I am so near

watching from a window
around the corner
a pigeon
who steps like a geisha girl
along a railing

looking away
at the moment she flies

I Used to Be Unbelievably Sexy

I used to be unbelievably sexy.
I was a rampant vine
that when you walk down the sidewalk
turns your head. You don't know
where the fragrance is coming from
but you peer and peer into the dark foliage.
It reminds you of being small and loose
in your grandmother's house. It reminds you
of accidental things, like wetting your pants,
so warm and sweet
until the remorse sets in.
I was the vine, but the bee, too,
that alights on that vine, greedy
to jam its feelers
down every syrupy throat.
I was running over with human sap.
I was a bare foot on rich black soil.
Now I'm tired as can be;
all I want is to sleep.
Now I see it was a trick:
nature's way of perpetuating the race.
But I refuse to be discarded,
to be the hapless ghost
of better days, my breasts hanging
like unwanted thumbs, womb collapsed
like a four-o'clock. What I've come down to
is something else:
the root under the vine,
the germ beneath the soil,
the skeletal foot inside the skin,
crisp as a blueprint and everlasting,

the delicate white bones of toes
that walk as they are meant to,
heartache or no heartache,
far into the next millennium.

Birthday Poem

Does the road wind past fields?
Silver in the rotted cups of fenceposts, snow
or moonlight; you no longer know the season.
Are the answers whole? Words are gravel
spinning from a tire. Your name? Forgotten,
or simply left behind in the long minnow's pull
through tunnels where your hair turns white; your voice,
receding, twists back into your mother's veins.
Color that has stained the nasturtiums
and thickened like a bruise on the eggplants
lifts from the garden at dusk, taken back
into the sun. Who is the sun?
Nothing now but particles of red or gold
in someone else's eye it grows
toward moonlight on a road
where gravel glistens.
A radio plays in a deserted parking lot
in the all-night laundromat's blue glare.

Brief Landing on the Earth's Surface

Even sometimes on a sidewalk
in the middle of everything
you feel it happening.
As though you were already moving on
the world recedes, the iron balconies
glitter like black sand
and the corners of tablecloths
lift and wave,
clairvoyant as handkerchiefs.